God's Foolishness

It sounds foolish, but don't be misled: this book is a little gem. From a man who has dedicated his life to God comes the wisdom of his years and a taste of the key influences in his life. There is wisdom and inspiration for everyone in these pages. If you have ever struggled with an absence of the experience of God in your prayer life, or are blindsided by despair for the future of our world, this book will help. A quick and easy read will have you looking up references and searching for more from the mystics Brian has featured. I highly recommend the book, particularly to those of us who yearn for, perhaps miss, the illusive experience of God.

Clare Shearman, spiritual director and host
The Cliffs Retreat, Shoreham, Vic.

God's Foolishness is accessible for those inquisitive or uncertain about spirituality from a Christian perspective, those who have been hurt by the Church but still desperately hungry for spiritual nourishment and healing, and for those people who long simply to move beyond the 'unfreedoms' experienced in our humanity. Brian's lens on God's wise foolishness, coupled with his deep insight into the human person through many years of vocational discernment and spiritual direction, serve to present these eight authors as real people encountering a loving God in their very real lives. Through each author Brian highlights that, however foolish we may consider ourselves, it is possible for God's love to become our own. From this perspective, we are invited to re-visit our hearts to discover an expansive love that frees us to stand compassionately inside our common humanity.

Janette Elliott, Registrar of Yarra Theological Union,
PhD Candidate, University of Divinity

This is an extraordinary book – extraordinary because it compresses into such a short space centuries of spiritual wisdom into which, perhaps, we have not yet fully immersed ourselves. Brian constantly reminds us that God longs to bless us, not condemn us. God is totally present to us in love, even when we experience darkness, weakness, failure, emptiness and powerlessness, be it individual or communal. When we focus on this infinite 'foolish' love of God for us, we are led to deep communion with and compassion for other people, whatever our religious tradition. *God's Foolishness* is inspiring, encouraging and filled with hope.

Paul Castley msc,
Spiritual director, supervisor, retreat giver.

A personal, compassionate and challenging reflection on the human experience of God cited at the beginning: *God's foolishness is wiser than human wisdom, and God's weakness is stronger than human strength.* We are drawn into wondering what this may mean in our own lives, by listening to the author's experience of the persistent call of God in his life and in the lives of several others in whom he sees reflected the same confronting and enticing truth: *the foolishness of God.*

Jill Manton, Founding Director of Wellspring Centre
Author of *An Ordinary Bloke: the Making of a Modern Mystic.*

A Spirituality of Heart

God's Foolishness

Brian Gallagher MSC

COVENTRY
PRESS

Published in Australia by
Coventry Press
33 Scoresby Road
Bayswater Vic. 3153
Australia

ISBN 9780648804468

Scripture quotations are from the *New Revised Standard Version Bible*,
copyright 1989, Division of Christian Education of the National Council
of the Churches of Christ in the United States of America. Used by
permission. All rights reserved.

Cataloguing-in-Publication entry is available from the National Library of
Australia http://catalogue.nla.gov.au/.

Cover design by Ian James - www.jgd.com.au
Text design by Megan Low (Film Shot Graphics FSG)
Typeset in Goudy Old Style

Printed in Australia

Contents

God's foolishness is wiser than human wisdom, and God's weakness is stronger than human strength. Consider your own call, brothers and sisters, not many of you were wise by human standards, not many were powerful, not many were of noble birth. But God chose what is foolish in the world to shame the wise; God chose what is weak in the world to shame the strong; God chose what is low and despised in the world, things that are not, to reduce to nothing things that are, so that no one might boast in the presence of God.

1 Corinthians 1:25-29

Introduction

Abandoning my studies in chemistry and metallurgy to enter the seminary seemed to many observers a radical change in life's direction. Even an irrational change! At the time (1962), I had recently finished a valuable research project and had good future prospects. I found it practically impossible to explain my decision to others – I am not sure that I understood it fully myself. Through the ups and downs of life, there were many subsequent times when I was invited to renew my commitment, but I didn't ever doubt that initial decision.

Perhaps all experiences of call seem like God's foolishness. I have witnessed hundreds of examples, as I watched fellow seminarians come and go over those early years, and, later, when I was ministering as a spiritual director. There is no second-guessing God's ways. This book reflects on the call of numerous others in history, people whose writings have been significant influences on my personal life. All seem to me to be further examples of God's foolish wisdom.

In my own case, the development of my call seems to me even greater foolishness on God's part. My life has been richly blessed, but it certainly hasn't been plain sailing! I often turn to Newman's *Lead Kindly Light* for inspiration:

> *So long thy power hath blessed me*
> *Sure it still will lead me on...*

Not unlike Paul's 'I know the one in whom I have put my trust.' (2 Timothy 1:12)

On a ministerial level, my first appointment after ordination was to teach science. No one was surprised, for I was surely well prepared for that. So much for human wisdom: after only six months, I moved into a new ministry of vocations promotion – with the advice and the encouragement of an older priest who mentored me at that time. This was doubtless the turning point of my life as a Missionary of the Sacred Heart, for vocations promotion quickly developed into youth work, retreat ministry, religious formation and spiritual direction, the last including two formative years in Boston in the mid-1970s and later, many years in the supervision and formation of other spiritual directors throughout Australia. I know that I have been well blessed in opportunities given to me, in community living, and in my ministry.

At the same time, on a personal level, the blessings were not always so obvious: for years, it was as if some battle was going on inside me. I know now that I was out of touch with my own inner life. I was struggling with vulnerabilities that I hadn't even named, a struggle that lasted for many years, and certainly affected my relationships. I thank God for the good help I received and for the gradual growth in awareness and inner freedom.

How reconcile these apparent opposite experiences – the fruitful ministry at the same time as the personal struggle within? It has been a sobering reminder that it is God's work that I do. Indeed, God's foolishness is wiser than human wisdom! The text continues:

> *God chose what is foolish in the world to shame the wise;*
> *God chose what is weak in the world to shame the strong.*

1 Corinthians 1:27-28

I don't hear Paul talking about different people – some wise, some foolish, some strong, some weak. Rather, it seems to me that God's choice of what is foolish and weak *in me* gives the lie to what I myself might have considered my wisdom or my strength. Time and time again, I have had to learn that my wisdom and my strength, *my* hard work and my prayer, count for precious little before God. There is nothing in me that can lay claim on God. I am utterly dependent on God's wisdom and strength. 'I know the one in whom I have put my trust.' (2 Timothy 1:12)

Indeed, once or twice, I have experienced that strength. Before God, I have experienced myself embraced, set free. I use the words of John of the Cross, the sixteenth century Carmelite mystic, who describes his experience:

> *You looked with love upon me*
> *And deep within your eyes imprinted grace;*
> *This mercy set me free,*

Held in your love's embrace,
To lift my eyes adoring to your face.[1]

Though the joy in such an experience doesn't necessarily last, the invitation is to keep believing that God's gift is ever present. For God is a self-giving God. All God knows is loving self-giving. With Karl Rahner and Denis Edwards, I call this 'God's self-bestowal'.

These theologians teach that from the beginning, God creates a world in which the Word is made flesh and the Spirit is poured out. The incarnation does not come about as a remedy for sin, as some theologies claim, but is central to God's creative act. The sending of the Spirit, often associated only with Pentecost, is equally central to God's creative act. 'Creation, redemption, and consummation are (thus) anchored in God's eternity.'[2] All are gifts of God's very self.

Believing that God's gift is ever-present, whatever of the inner experience, challenged Thomas Merton to describe his prayer in this way: 'my prayer is centered on faith... a kind of praise rising up out of the centre of nothingness and silence'. *A kind of praise* makes good sense to me: a mixture of gratitude and wonder, bowing before God – yes, praising God.

Traditional teaching in spirituality teaches that when little seems to be happening in prayer – 'nothingness and silence' – such apparent emptiness, in fact, is fullness. Hence

---

1   John of the Cross, *Spiritual Canticle*, stanza 32. This translation is taken from Iain Matthew, *The Impact of God* (London: Hodder & Stoughton, 1995), 29
2   Catherine Mowry LaCugna, *God for Us: The Trinity and Christian Life* (New York: HarperOne, 1991), 209.

John of the Cross: 'nothingness is all'[3] and *The Cloud of Unknowing*: 'unknowing is to know'.[4] Then I remember 'my power is made perfect in weakness' (2 Corinthians 12:9): to know my weakness is my strength. The experience doesn't feel any less empty or weak, but it is an experience of God. Seen with different eyes, I believe that the emptiness is somehow transformed – not taken away, but imbued with new hope. John says, with love. How 'foolish' is that! This foolishness permeates what follows.

Indeed, my choice of the authors who have influenced me may seem foolish enough – let alone their lives and their teachings. Human wisdom says there is no way in which that bohemian Tom Merton can become a monk! Nor can that high society lady in Avila, Teresa, become a nun and a reformer! And Etty Hillesum is just another insignificant Jewish girl – nothing will come of her life! Martin Luther King is just another oppressed black man: so be it! Human wisdom says that Jules Chevalier is doing a good job in his remote country parish, thank you: leave him there. Maybe Constance Fitzgerald is an exception, but surely she should stay in her monastery instead of all that tripping around the world! So should that rebel Sebastian Moore!

As I explain in what follows, God's foolishness saw these women and men with very different eyes. The amount of written material available on each and, in some instances,

---

3   John of the Cross, *The Ascent of Mount Carmel* in *The Collected Works of St. John of the Cross* (Washington, DC: Institute of Carmelite Studies, 1973), Book I, 13, 11.

4   *The Cloud of Unknowing* (New York: Doubleday, 1973).

the complexity of their teaching, results in chapters of varying lengths.

I praise the God whose foolishness is wiser by far than my poor wisdom.

Jules Chevalier

Jules Chevalier (1824-1907) was parish priest of Issoudun, a small country village in France. Inspired by the plight of neglected country people, Chevalier began missionary work in Issoudun. The work expanded as other priests joined him, to the point where in 1854 Chevalier founded the religious congregation of the Missionaries of the Sacred Heart. After some years, as foolish as it seemed in 1881, Chevalier accepted the Holy See's invitation to send missionaries to Papua New Guinea. The rest is history: Missionaries of the Sacred Heart now number over 2000 priests and brothers, and countless associated sisters and lay people, ministering in twenty-five countries.

Another of the poems of John of the Cross is called *The Living Flame of Love*. This is the last verse:

> *Your fragrant breathing stills me*
> *Your grace, your glory fills me*
> *So tenderly, your love becomes my own.*[5]

---

5   John of the Cross, *Centred on Love: the Poems of St. John of the Cross* translated by Marjorie Flower (Varroville NSW 2565: the Carmelite Nuns, 1983, reprinted 2002), 23.

'Your love becomes my own' could well have been the inspiration for Jules Chevalier's writing. Two favourite Scripture texts of Chevalier were:

> *In this is love: not that we loved God, but that he loved us.*
> *We love because God first loved us.* 1 John 4:10, 19

This love of God was revealed to us in the Heart of Jesus. In Chevalier's own words:

> *The heart of Jesus is the heart of God,*
> *the centre of divine love,*
> *the means by which the Incarnate Word loves us...*
> *In this heart, God gives himself completely.*
> *Yes, God gives himself completely.*
> *God who is wholly love*
> *experiences a hunger and thirst to give himself...*
> *God wants to overflow and spread himself.*[6]

This is the love of God that Chevalier lived, preached and shared with other people. With Chevalier, we believe and live that 'God's love has been poured into our hearts through the Holy Spirit that has been given to us' (Romans 5:5), indeed 'God is love' (I John 4:8). All God knows is to love: God gives Godself to us in creation, in incarnation, in the life of grace (the gift of the Spirit), and in final fulfillment.[7] In his personal

---

6 Jules Chevalier, *The Sacred Heart* (Paris: Retaux-Bray, 1886, republished 1900), 277. I have kept the original exclusive language.

7 Later theologies call God's gift of Godself 'God's self-bestowal', 'a Trinitarian act of self-bestowal'. See, for example, Denis Edwards, *How God Acts: Creation, Redemption and Special Divine Action* (Hindmarsh SA: ATF Theology, 2010), 39.

life and in the spirituality he developed, Chevalier focuses on God's loving self-giving: 'your love becomes my own'. This is the foundation of his legacy.

Even in the religious communities which Chevalier founded, this foundational truth was lost sight of for many years. The explanation of this is found in the history of religious life.

Two major influences in that history have been the Rule of St Benedict and the Spiritual Exercises of St Ignatius. In his Rule, St Benedict asked his monks for regular 'manifestation of conscience' to the Abbot or to a wise elder. This was meant to be separate from confession (reconciliation), but its effect was to emphasise the external practices of living religious life or keeping the rule. The main focus of religious life became a person's behaviour, not their relationship with God or their inner life, not God's love and God's call. This overflowed into most other religious congregations.

Later, the Spiritual Exercises of St Ignatius became very popular in religious formation. Though it was not Ignatius' intention, what happened was that many treated Ignatius' account of his religious experience as a series of prayer exercises that other people were expected to undergo. Again, the focus became more on the externals, not the prayer experience. For example, Ignatius encouraged the prayer called the Consciousness Examen, listening contemplatively to God's presence and invitation in one's daily life. His focus was on God's gift and God's invitation. Somehow, this became an Examination of Conscience, focusing rather on what I have done well and done poorly during each day, missing Ignatius' intention.

It seems to me that this focus on external behaviour dominated for years in religious life, in Christian life, in preaching and in teaching. Maybe there are elements of it with us still. The centrality of God's love, God loving us first, was lost.

If living our life focuses on behaviour only, little real growth happens. Personal development or growth cannot be forced, only facilitated and supported. A focus on external behaviour does not address the underlying personal issues around the deeper places within a person that determine their behaviour. There is a well established psychology around the human experience of inner freedom that supports this understanding of personal growth. I discuss below the human experience of limited freedom: though we are essentially free, created free, effectively, we are also unfree, the experience well described by Paul:

> *I do not understand my own actions.*
> *For I do not do what I want, but I do the very things I hate...*
> *I can will what is right, but I cannot do it.*
> *For I do not do the good I want,*
> *but the evil I do not want is what I do.*

Romans 7:15, 18-19

Why do we sometimes find ourselves doing what we really don't want to do? Because there is something else in us, deeper inside our make-up, that is not free. And so, our motivation is mixed. Only God's love can set us free. Focus on behaviour alone will not bring about any growth in inner freedom.

John of the Cross' poem *Spiritual Canticle* that I cited in the Introduction speaks of this, too:

> *You looked with love upon me*
> *this mercy set me free*
> *held in your love's embrace*
> *to lift my eyes adoring to you face.*[8]

Only God's love sets us free. In the experience of God's looking upon us with love, we are set free. Convinced of this, Jules Chevalier wrote that God's love, revealed in the Heart of Jesus, is the answer to all ills in the world, what he called the *mal moderne*. I'm sure Chevalier would have included all the personal 'ills' – the ills inside our hearts – as much as the ills in society. He knew that when we know God's love in our lives, then we are healed and freed. This overflows into our relationships – we become more compassionate and caring of other people.

Jules Chevalier wrote extensively in books and letters, but most of his writing was overlooked in the early years of the societies he founded. It is not uncommon, apparently, that a Founder's vision for the religious group that he begins is not fully appreciated initially. Chevalier's initial *Constitutions* were drastically revised by an early General Chapter of his congregation, for example, omitting his insistence that

---

8   John of the Cross, *Spiritual Canticle*, stanza 32.

devotion to the Sacred Heart was the remedy for the ills of the time. His *Constitutions* were reclaimed only in later years and his foundational spirituality was studied and gradually appreciated more by his religious family.

Chevalier's expression of God's self-bestowal – 'Your love becomes my own' – is captured in several passages in his writings. For example:

> *His heart is the sacred bond*
> *uniting heaven and earth*
> *and binding all things to the One*
> *from whom everything flows.*
>
> *In this heart, God gives himself completely.*
> *Yes, God gives himself completely.*
> *God who is wholly love*
> *experiences a hunger and thirst to give himself...*
>
> *God wants to overflow and spread himself.*
> *And he has overflowed onto the world*
> *through his Word made flesh.*
> *It is through the heart of Christ*
> *that the love of God, God himself,*
> *pours himself out on the world and on the human race.*[9]

The move back to a focus on the love of God in our hearts has been given a boost in recent times by Pope Francis. In his encyclical *Laudato Si* (2015) on the care for our common home, Pope Francis stresses God's love for all people and all creation

---

9 Jules Chevalier, *The Sacred Heart*, 277.

in sentences like 'God's love is the fundamental moving force in all created things' and 'Every creature is the object of the Father's tenderness.' (#77) The Pope's emphasis on the interconnectedness of all creation – which includes all people – united in God's love, is the foundation of his ecological theology. In recent times, it has given encouragement also to a feminist theology, acknowledging the equality of all people, men and women. It is the foundation, too, of a heart spirituality, the way of the heart, care for others and concern for justice for all.

Thomas Merton

Thomas Merton (1915-1968) was an American Trappist monk in the Abbey of Gethsemani in Kentucky. Though Merton would have been judged by many to be quite unsuited for a strict enclosed monastic life, he was accepted as a novice in 1942. Merton would become a celebrated writer and poet, publishing over seventy books as well as numerous articles and journals. He is regarded as one of the foremost writers of the century. In 1968, Merton attended an inter-religious conference in Bangkok, Thailand, where he died accidently.

When a young Tom Merton presented himself at the gates of the Trappist monastery called Our Lady of Gethsemani (near the small town of Bardstown in Kentucky) in December 1941, he would have had precious little knowledge of the monastic life-style to which he aspired. Certainly he would have read extensively, and he would have witnessed something of the monks' prayer life from the distance of the guest house on a weekend visit earlier in the year, but Merton's own life experience could not have been more different from that of the monks at Gethsemani.

Merton was 26 years old, by all accounts, an unsettled young man. Both his parents were deceased, and he was not particularly close to his only brother, four years younger than himself. He belonged to a circle of university friends, having graduated from Columbia University and at the time was teaching at Bonaventure University in New York. He was a literary buff, a writer and journalist, whose life-style many described as rather bohemian. His recent conversion to Catholicism, lengthy inner struggles with Church and vocation, and a number of significant religious experiences had led Merton to see his call to the monastic life.

Such a way of life - enclosed and strictly structured - was utterly different from anything in Merton's previous experience. It comes as no surprise that he struggled with it for years. But Gethsemani was the place and the lifestyle that Merton had chosen quite freely, believing that this was God's call for him - that here, in this place, he would discover and know God, that in this place, he would live happily and fruitfully in relation to God and his brother monks.

Such an expectation was quite understandable; indeed, monastic life, with vows of stability and simplicity, poverty, chastity and obedience, in a community whose rule and routine is built around the sanctification of the day and its activities, is a traditionally acknowledged way to God. Merton may well have expected that the many hours of the monk's day spent in prayer - the communal Prayer of the Church and the personal prayer called *Lectio Divina* - in such an apparently peaceful and silent environment in every way conducive to contemplation, would bring him close to God.

What happened, in fact, was quite different and quite unexpected. Initially, I discuss what was arguably the core mystical experience of Merton's life. I then draw out three themes which I call 'illusion-shatterers'.

Merton, now known as Brother Louis, records the first two occasions when he left the confines of the monastic enclosure to visit Louisville, the closest larger town to Gethsemani. The first – his very first excursion 'into the world' – was in 1948, seven years after he had entered Gethsemani. He wrote:

> I found that everything stirred me with a deep and mute sense of compassion... I went through the city, realising for the first time in my life how good are all the people in the world and how much value they have in the sight of God. After that I returned to the peaceful routine of the monastic life – I had only left it for six hours.[10]

The second, ten years later, 1958, was even more significant. In Merton's own words:

> On the corner of a busy street in Louisville... I was suddenly overwhelmed with the realisation that I loved all of these people... I suddenly saw the secret beauty of their hearts which neither sin nor desire nor self-knowledge can reach, the core of their reality, the person that each one is in God's eyes. If only they could all see themselves as they really are.[11]

---

10 Thomas Merton, *The Sign of Jonas* (New York: Harcourt, Brace and Co., 1953), 91-92.

11 Thomas Merton, *Conjectures of a Guilty Bystander* (New York: Doubleday, 1966), 156-158.

I see this experience as the turning point of Merton's life, radically transforming his whole life.[12]

Merton's self-image

This is the first illusion to be shattered: whatever of all the years of faithful monastic observance, designed to promote religious experience, in fact, Merton's pivotal experience happens on a busy street corner, surrounded by hundreds of people he had never met. As one commentator pictured it, 'while waiting for a traffic light to change in the middle of the shopping centre'.

The inescapable message is that being a monk is not what counts before God, so much as being human, being part of the human race. What matters before God is not what differentiates us from others but what inseparably unites us. Go back to the monastery, certainly, but no longer because the monastery is a privileged place to know God, but because there, as a monk, you are called to live your humanity to the full. Becoming and living your true self was to become a recurring theme of Merton's writing. He taught that we are all called to be mystics – in the sense of living our lives authentically and lovingly.

Merton is quick to emphasise that being true to oneself is not as simple as it sounds – 'because', he says, 'every one of us is shadowed by a false self'. He explains this in his work *New Seeds of Contemplation*:

---

12 This discussion of Merton's experience is based on my article in *Mystics for Every Millennium* (Canterbury, Vic: Heart of Life, 2002).

> *Every one of us is shadowed by a false self. This is the man I want myself to be, but who cannot exist because God doesn't know anything about him. And to be unknown to God is altogether too much privacy. My false and private self is the one who wants to exist outside the reach of God's will and God's love – outside of reality and outside of life. Such a self cannot help but be an illusion.*[13]

My true self, on the other hand, is the self that God created, loves and sustains. As Merton said in describing his experience on the street corner, our true self is 'the person each one of us is in God's eyes'. Indeed, God constantly calls us to the truth of our self: in any honest prayer, in any honest relationship, God invites us and challenges us to face our inner attachments, the untruths of the false self, and to discover and live our true self. Merton taught that this is impossible in isolation from God, indeed in isolation from the rest of humanity. Which are my second and third themes.

Merton in relation to all humanity

The book in which Merton described his mystical experience on the street corner in Louisville is called *Conjectures of a Guilty Bystander*. The title tells us of Merton's guilt around being an observer of human affairs (from his monastic seclusion), rather than an involved participant. This guilt surely changes, just as his lifestyle changes, after the Louisville experience.

---

13   Thomas Merton, *New Seeds of Contemplation* (New York: New Direction Books, 1961), 161.

The first and unavoidable corollary of the invitation to be oneself, to be human, is to be involved with other human people. This is the second illusion-shatterer: the enclosed contemplative monk who, in his own words, opted to 'leave the world', to be utterly detached from the world, found himself deeply involved in the important issues of the so-called 'world' outside of his monastery. This was not Merton's initial vision of his call to monastic life, but he found that he could no longer remain uninvolved, so strong was his compassion and sense of oneness with God's people. Later, he was to say that he was 'in a state of ecstasy' in relation to the human race.

In his own lifetime and in his enduring writings, Merton became a highly respected commentator and leader in movements for social action and transformation – civil rights, non-violence, peace and justice for all people.

Merton's sense of belonging and commitment to all of God's people seems to me to be the surest sign of the validity of his experience in Louisville. Even for the contemplative monk, what God gives us is to be shared. Mystical experience asks a forgetting of oneself – for the sake of others. Caring for others, compassion in relationships with others, is both fruit and test of religious experience.

Merton's relationship with God

Living one's humanity truthfully and fully will also mean coming to know God more truthfully. In his book *Spiritual Direction and Meditation*, Merton wrote:

> *A contemplative is not one who takes his prayer seriously, but*
> *one who takes God seriously... one who is famished for truth,*
> *who seeks to live in generous simplicity, in the spirit.*[14]

Here is the third surprise, the third illusion to be shattered: to take God seriously, to make God our first concern and focus, means that our prayer will look after itself. For Merton, it seems that taking God seriously means that all of our effort, all of our earnestness, even our desire for God counts for little. The greatest illusion is to imagine that the years of hard work, prayer and asceticism, will necessarily give some claim on God's gift of intimacy.

When he returned to the monastery after the Louisville experience, Merton's experience of God changed radically. This experience is captured in his book *Contemplative Prayer*, published just after his untimely death. Readers may well have expected to read about a contented life of contemplative prayer, sustained by some comforting sense of God's presence, the consolation of inner peace and joy. But no. Merton wrote about *dread*:

> *Dread is an expression of our insecurity in this earthly life...*
>
> *The full maturity of the spiritual life cannot be reached unless*
> *we first pass through the dread and anguish, the trouble and fear*
> *that necessarily accompany the inner crisis of 'spiritual death'*
> *in which we finally abandon our attachment to our exterior self*
> *and surrender completely to Christ.*[15]

14   Thomas Merton, *Spiritual Direction and Meditation* (Collegeville: Liturgical Press, 1960), 33.

15   Thomas Merton, *Contemplative Prayer* (New York: Herder & Herder, 1969), 101.

Dread is the experience of knowing deep in our heart that we can never be completely sure of ourselves, our wisdom, our prayer, our fidelity. Merton teaches rather that we find God – and know God truly – only in the awareness of our nothingness. It sounds morbid, but for Merton it was painfully, wonderfully liberating. God's foolishness?

This experience places Merton in the apophatic way, sometimes called the *way of negation*. It is a way in spirituality that is strictly without images, without words. Images are negated or set aside for the sake of knowing God who is beyond all imagining. Even years before writing *Contemplative Prayer*, Merton had recognised that the purifying, illuminating, transforming experience of God is in *darkness*, a divine darkness that can be described only as light. Merton once used the image of being in a completely dark room, not able to see, hear, feel, anything but utter darkness, but still knowing that someone else is in the room. This is the sense in which Merton believes that we can 'know' God.

With this experience, Merton found himself looking to Asia, to the so-called 'East', where the apophatic tradition is commonly taken for granted. He was particularly attracted to Zen. Zen talks of 'self-emptying' as the way to the experience of our 'essential nature' and our oneness with all being, all people, all nature, a theme that will recur in this book.

This was Merton's experience at those traffic lights in Louisville:

I was suddenly overwhelmed by the realisation that I loved all of these people... I suddenly saw the secret beauty of their hearts... the core of their reality, the person that each one is in God's eyes.[16]

Only a week before he died, Merton visited Polonnaruwa in Sri Lanka. He was totally captivated by a local shrine – two massive Buddha figures, one seated, one reclining ('carved not by ordinary mortals', said one of Merton's guides). This is Merton's own account of his experience. It seems to me to be the complement of the earlier Louisville experience:

> *Looking at these figures, I was suddenly, almost forcibly, jerked clean out of the habitual, half-tired vision of things – an inner clearness, clarity, as if exploding from the rocks themselves, became evident and obvious... there is no puzzle, no problem, and really no "mystery"... I have now seen and have pierced through the surface – I've got beyond the shadow and the disguise...*[17]

Merton describes, from his own experience – in Louisville and Polonnaruwa – what Zen calls the *Essential Nature* of all reality. Perhaps what Christianity would call the indwelling Spirit in all reality. This simple, mystical vision of reality, of oneself and all creation, in God, is Merton's legacy, fruit of his seemingly irrational response to God's call years earlier.

'Consider your own call, brothers and sisters... God chose what is foolish in the world to shame the wise; God chose what is weak in the world to shame the strong... so that

---

16 Thomas Merton, *Conjectures of a Guilty Bystander*, 156.
17 Thomas Merton, *Asian Journal* (New York: New Direction Books, 1973), 233-235.

no one might boast in the presence of God.' Thomas Merton is a classic example of Paul's teaching in 1 Corinthians.

Etty Hillesum

Etty Hillesum (1914-1943) was a young Jewish Dutch woman who kept diaries and wrote letters to friends during her time in Westerbork, a transit camp in the Netherlands, the last stop before Auschwitz. She died in Auschwitz on 30 November 1943. To all appearances, Etty's background and life-style prior to her move to Westerbork would seem at odds with the mystical experience she recorded in her diaries.

Etty Hillesum was an unusual young woman, highly intellectual, well qualified academically, and deeply compassionate. The last words in her diary are 'we should be willing to act as balm for all wounds.'[18] Etty was not only willing, but she saw herself called to speak and write on behalf of hundreds of Jewish people who were living in the concentration camp. Her sense of solidarity with Jewish people and ultimately with all humanity overflowed into her daily care for others in the camp:

---

18 Etty Hillesum, *Etty: A Diary 1941-1943* (London: Triad Grafton Books, 1985), 251.

I was sometimes filled with an infinite tenderness, and lay awake for hours letting the many, too many impressions of a much too long day wash over me, and I prayed 'Let me be the thinking heart of these barracks'.[19]

That experience of solidarity or oneness with humanity, I believe, came from Etty's personal experience of God in her life. In her words:

To think that one small human heart can experience so much, oh my God, so much suffering and so much love. I am so grateful to You, God, for having chosen my heart in these times to experience all the things it has experienced... And talking to you, God. Is that alright? With the passing of people, I feel a growing need to speak to You alone. I love people so terribly, because in every human being, I love something of You. And I seek You everywhere in them, and often do find something of You.[20]

Etty seemed well aware that she was being led into the hearts of other people. Her sense of deep communion with humanity and with the cosmos came as gift. Others come to similar awareness in quiet prayer or through theological reflection on God's love for all. For Etty Hillesum, it came from her compassion - her desire to be balm - for her persecuted people:

There among the barracks full of hunted and persecuted people, I found confirmation of my love of life... Not for one moment

---

19 Ibid, 245.
20 Ibid, 217.

was I cut off from life. There was simply one great meaningful whole. Will I be able to describe all that one day? So that others can feel, too, how lovely and worth living and just – yes, just – life really is.[21]

Etty Hillesum was not particularly religious. In her early life, she seemed little aware of even her Jewish background and heritage, though this changed as she met more Jewish people after leaving her family home. Her asking God was it 'alright' to talk with God eventually became what Etty called 'an uninterrupted dialogue' with God:

You have made me so rich, oh God... My life has become an uninterrupted dialogue with You, oh God, one great dialogue. Sometimes when I stand in some corner of the camp, my feet planted on Your earth, my eyes raised toward Your heaven, tears sometimes run down my face, tears of deep emotion and gratitude. At night, too, when I lie in my bed and rest in You, oh God, tears of gratitude run down my face and that is my prayer.[22]

It is this that I call Etty Hillesum's mystical experience, her intimate contact with God, the God she met in every other person. Just as she lived her life, Etty doubtless faced her death in this same spirit of deep gratitude to God, in solidarity with and on behalf of her people.

---

21 Ibid. 229.
22 Etty Hillesum in Jan G. Gaarlandt, ed., *Letters from Westerbork* (London: Grafton Books, 1988), 116. The letter sent to her friend Tide (Henny Tideman) was dated 18 August 1943.

Lady Wisdom

The author of the fourteenth century classic called *The Cloud of Unknowing* is not known. The anonymous author, I suspect, is a woman, not revealing her identity in days when female writers were discouraged, even forbidden, in the early church. Personally, I stand her alongside other wisdom figures in our tradition – the author of the Bible's Book of Wisdom, *Sophia*, and the traditional Celtic crone, all female. I call her Lady Wisdom.

The Cloud of Unknowing stands out in spirituality literature for its different approach to God and to prayer. Written from the prayer experience of the author, in the *Cloud*, Lady Wisdom teaches that we come to know God, indeed to know truth, by *unknowing*:

> *The most God-like knowledge of God is that which is known by unknowing.*[23]

> *This is what you are to do: lift your heart up to the Lord, with a gentle stirring love, desiring him for his own sake and not for his gifts. Centre all your attention and your desire on him... In*

---

23 Anon. *The Cloud of Unknowing* #70.

the beginning, it is usual to feel a kind of darkness about your mind, or as it were, a cloud of unknowing. *You will seem to know nothing and to feel nothing except a naked intent toward God in the depths of your being... Learn to be at home in this darkness.*[24]

Two centuries later, John of the Cross wrote:

Nothing which could possibly be imagined or comprehended in this life can be a proximate means of union with God.[25]

This is the apophatic way in spirituality. As discussed in an earlier chapter, the apophatic way seeks to deny or negate anything and everything that is not God, in its focus on the God who is ever beyond our minds and our hearts, the God who is ineffable, nameless, utter mystery, the God who can be loved, but not fully known. Because God is God.

Our desire to know God, not merely the gifts of God, asks us to put aside all else, all thinking, all good insight, all cosy feeling, precisely because it is God that we long for. Putting all else aside ultimately leaves us in emptiness or darkness, as described by *The Cloud* and by other authors in the same tradition. This is God's foolishness at its best/worst.

There are numerous well-proven helps to relaxing the body, stilling the mind, and staying focused. The practice of Zen meditation, for example, is designed to help not only with concentration and stillness, but also with perspective on God. Zen is defined simply as 'contemplation', practised by

---

24 Ibid. chapter 3.
25 John of the Cross, *Ascent of Mount Carmel* II, 8, 4.

regular sitting meditation and the daily habit of mindfulness (being fully present to the here and now). As discussed fully in my book *The Eyes of God*,[26] Zen practice hopes for some enlightenment, the realisation of what Zen calls one's 'essential nature', one's deep inner truth, one with all God's creation. Thomas Merton, who practised Zen meditation for a time, wrote that 'the deepest level of communication is not communication, but communion'.[27] Communion, sharing in the life of God.

I know the experience of emptiness or darkness in my prayer. I don't use many words when I pray: I tend to 'just sit'– as the Zen teachers say – usually with a mantra to give me a focus and help keep me in the present moment. I cannot claim any strong awareness of God, but on some level, I seem to know that what I am doing is worthwhile. Indeed, I find that I want to do it, I want to pray. I want God. My desire for God leaves me in a place of patient/impatient waiting. Contemplative prayer involves waiting. This is the unknowing that Lady Wisdom speaks of.

Because such communion is beyond words and beyond concept, it's true that the prayer seems quite empty in the praying. I seem to have precious little to show for the time I give to prayer. Benedictine Abbot John Chapman says that the prayer time is so empty that 'it felt like the completest waste of time'.[28] I once said that it felt more like God's absence

---

26 Brian Gallagher, *The Eyes of God* (Bayswater Vic: Coventry Press, 2019), 36, 41-42.

27 Thomas Merton, *Asian Journal*, 308.

28 John Chapman, *Spiritual Letters* (London: Sheed & Ward, 1983). Appendix.

than God's presence. To which my spiritual director replied '... only because you are imagining God's presence has to be always warm and comforting'. No longer! As mentioned in my Introduction, Karl Rahner wrote that 'emptiness is fullness'. Unknowing is knowing. To persevere in such prayer asks deep faith, a faith which Merton said was the core of his prayer.

We share in the life of God not only in times of prayer. Zen is a way of life, contemplation is a way of life. Wisdom literature sees God's life in 'the structures of the world and the activity of the elements... the alternation of the solstices and the changes of the seasons, the cycles of the year and the constellations of the stars... the varieties of plants and the virtues of roots'. (Wisdom 7:17-20) I believe in that presence: God is present in all life, all creation, all human experience. Indeed, I have sensed something of that life of God in those wonderfully gifted times when crossing the vast empty Nullabor and when cruising the pristine-pure Gordon and Franklin rivers: it's as though I'm swallowed up by creation. I become one with God's creation. I lose awareness of my self as separate and observing.

Wisdom and compassion are the bulwarks of Zen: wisdom to see and know oneself truly and to see and know all reality truly, compassion to know one's identity with all reality. The same wisdom and compassion are the fruits of the contemplative prayer taught by The Cloud of Unknowing. None of which makes sense to human wisdom. God's foolishness.

I note that, in contrast to the apophatic way, what is called the kataphatic way uses images and words to approach God. The kataphatic way acknowledges the many gifts of God, the gifts of God's creation, and sees these as ways to God. In the kataphatic way, one's prayer tends to be more discursive, often using words and images. Lady Wisdom teaches that both the apophatic and the kataphatic ways are valid, complementary ways to God. Indeed, the *Cloud of Unknowing* recommends the use of words and images in prayer, when appropriate and when possible. For example, many people find themselves happy to join in the singing and celebration of liturgical prayer, even though their personal prayer times seem empty of celebration. Each not only complements, but supports the other.

Martin Luther King

Martin Luther King (1929-1968) was an American Baptist minister who became a prominent leader in the civil rights movement. Preaching non-violence and civil disobedience, King was awarded the Nobel Peace Prize in 1964. King found his inspiration in the experience of his own youth, having grown up in the segregated city of Atlanta and suffering from daily discrimination. Martin Luther King was assassinated in 1968.

In 1963, an American black man called Martin Luther King stood on the steps of the Lincoln Memorial in Washington and addressed the thousands of African-American people who had marched from all parts of the country in the cause of their freedom. Martin Luther King's speech, *I have a dream*, has gone down in history as a turning point in the American story. This is King's dream:

> *I say to you today, my friends, so even though we face the difficulties of today and tomorrow, I still have a dream. It is a dream deeply rooted in the American dream.*

I have a dream that one day this nation will rise up and live out the true meaning of its creed: 'We hold these truths to be self-evident – that all men are created equal'.

I have a dream that one day on the red hills of Georgia, the sons of former slaves and the sons of former slave owners will be able to sit down together at a table of brotherhood.

I have a dream that one day even the state of Mississippi, a state sweltering with the heat of injustice, sweltering with the heat of oppression, will be transformed into an oasis of freedom and justice.

I have a dream that my four little children will one day live in a nation where they will not be judged by the colour of their skin, but by the content of their character.

I have a dream today.

I have a dream that one day every valley shall be exalted, every hill and mountain shall be made low, the rough places will be made plain and the crooked places will be made straight, and the glory of the Lord shall be revealed, and all flesh shall see it together.

Martin Luther King's dream held both challenge and hope for his people. At the same time, he spoke to all people.

In my listening, King's first message is that our dreams are not solely for ourselves. Our dreams are meant to be shared and passed on. Our dreams are given to us for the sake of all God's people. Our dreams have potential to change people.

The same Martin Luther King once said that 'the Church is the place you go out from'. Life is to be shared, our blessings in life are to be shared, our dreams are to be shared. We do well to listen to one another's dreams.

The other learning for me, as I listen to Martin Luther King again, is that our dreams don't die. Our dreams are somehow universal; they are picked up elsewhere. In his popular song *Imagine*, John Lennon wrote 'You may say I'm a dreamer – but I'm not the only one!' Our dreams don't die. Our dreams are always relevant – indeed, there are still oppressed people in our world. I believe our dreams are gift; they are an expression of God's dream. Dreams are sometimes called 'the language of God'. God speaks to us and invites us to growth via our dreams. Which is the importance of listening to our dreams.

Our dreams bring to the surface our hopes and our prayers on behalf of all humanity. 'Your old men shall dream dreams and your young men shall see visions.' (Joel 2:28) Whether old or young, I believe that we dream the dreams that challenge us all to care for one another and to take a stand against injustice and oppression in our world. As Martin Luther King reminds us, our dreams are not solely for ourselves.

Constance Fitzgerald

Constance Fitzgerald is a Carmelite Sister in USA. She is a prominent exponent of Carmelite spirituality, in particular through her study of the Carmelite mystics John of the Cross and Teresa of Avila. Though a member of an enclosed monastery, Fitzgerald travels widely to offer lectures and workshops.

The Church in Australia is severely bruised as she slowly comes to terms with revelations of scandal, abuse and cover-up. This has impacted on reduced numbers of attendees in parishes and loss of standing in the community. At the same time, society as a whole is struggling, overwhelmed by a population explosion, an unprecedented humanitarian crisis of refugees, inequality of resources, the fear of terrorism and nuclear war, and a damaged earth and environment.

Confronted by many questions and few answers, the surprise is that something new may well be emerging in our world and in our church.

Constance Fitzgerald was the first to recognise that the personal experience that John of the Cross calls a 'dark night' happens also on a communal level – in society, in Church, and in communities. She named the experience *impasse*, when there appears no way out, no rational escape, and no turning back from the situation in which we find ourselves. Indeed, when the temptation for some is to give up, to surrender to despair and hopelessness. But, writes Fitzgerald:

> *what if, by chance, our time in evolution is a 'dark night' time – a time of crisis and transition that must be understood if it is to be part of learning a new vision and harmony for the human species and the planet?*[29]

John of the Cross discovered that, paradoxically, a situation of no potential is loaded with potential.[30] John's teaching about the dark night is that in the very experience of darkness and joylessness, in the suffering and withdrawal of the satisfaction and pleasure we were accustomed to, a transformation is taking place. Dark night means new life, an experience of grace, of consolation (admittedly that does not necessarily feel very consoling). John says it is a time when we are being purified, when egoism dies and unselfish love for another is set free, when we are challenged to move from loving and serving others because of the joy it gives us, to loving and serving others for their sake, regardless of the cost to ourselves. It is a time of deepening relationship with God, indeed deepening of all our relationships.

---

29 Constance Fitzgerald, 'Impasse and Dark Night' in Tilden Edwards, ed. *Living with Apocalypse*, (San Francisco, CA: Harper & Row, 1984), 94.
30 John of the Cross, 'Dark Night' in Kieran Kavanaugh and Otilio Rodriguez eds, *The Collected Works of St. John of the Cross*, (Washington, DC: Institute of Carmelite Studies, 1973).

Fitzgerald's original writing was in 1984. She wrote what she calls an 'update' in 2009, reinforcing her earlier understanding of John of the Cross and updating her examples of communal impasse. Whereas in 1984, Fitzgerald wrote of the 'purification of our desires' as a gift of grace freeing us for new life and new mission, later she adds, also from John of the Cross, the 'purification of our memories'.[31]

She writes of the tension between remembering and forgetting. There are experiences in life that we remember vividly – indeed, we dare not forget because of their significance for us. And yet, in another sense, we are invited to forget them, to leave them behind in order to be open to new experience. Fitzgerald says we want 'to be receptive to transformative hope'. This does not mean ignoring our memories, but rather an 'unravelling or de-linking' of our memories. John of the Cross calls this 'purification of memory': purification frees us from the hold our memories have on us. John and Constance Fitzgerald note that we too easily become attached to our memories, which then block the development of our relationship with God and our relationships with other people. The problem is that 'memories can lead us either to healing and empathy or to hostility and destruction'. Only when 'purified' will our memories ensure the former.

I think of personal examples. When I remember times when I have been deeply hurt, I don't imagine I will ever forget them. But the risk is that I could become bitter and revengeful, unless I do forget in some way, unless I am open to

31 Constance Fitzgerald, *From Impasse to Prophetic Hope: Crisis of Memory*, Catholic Theological Society of America, vol. 64, 2009.

transformative hope. Only then will I grow in empathy.

In 2009, Fitzgerald's examples were the horrendous evil inflicted upon the Jewish people in the holocaust, the genocide in Bosnia and other parts of the world, and the systemic injustice of women's experience of social and ecclesial marginalisation. She says, 'I strive to be faithful in solidarity with those who continue to remember indescribable violation and at the same time I am receptive to the transforming power of hope that deconstructs memory'.

In an article I wrote for the National Council of Priests, I discussed Fitzgerald's articles in relation to the present *impasse* around the Church's history of sexual abuse.[32] We must remember- indeed we cannot afford to forget – our sin and the pain inflicted on thousands of young people, still often unhealed. There is no turning back from this reality. As a Church, we have committed ourselves to more careful accountability and to strict ethical norms of behaviour, but I believe that the real conversion has to be within our personal and communal hearts.

Fitzgerald says this is a 'radical call', asking us to leave much behind. It may be quite painful because it is a time of dark emptiness, calling on deep faith, as we face the reality of the impasse we are in. Any hope comes from our acceptance of the painful memories of the Church's past, rather than imagining some 'back to normal' dream. We are invited, rather, to 'deconstruct' our memories, to see them differently, but never to forget them.

32 Brian Gallagher, *The Swag* (Journal of the National Council of Priests, Australia) 26, no. 2, 2018, 17-18.

Fitzgerald believes that the dynamic of purification of memories will come about in a person's prayer, which she calls the prayer of silent waiting on God, a prayer which 'radically changes a person and opens into new possibilities, new vision, a vast bottomless and incomprehensible Future toward which hope reaches and love gives'.

In prayer, we acknowledge that we are limited and powerless to change what is happening for us, communally in society and Church, and that we are willing to surrender to the mystery, the unknown future, waiting on the gift of God. As we face that uncertain future, doubtless with mixed emotion, the new life in our dying will surely emerge. As foolish and unlikely as this sounds, we are being invited to trust God's wisdom.

Teresa of Avila

Teresa of Avila (1515-1582) was a Spanish noblewoman living an active social life before her call to join the monastic life of the Carmelite sisters in the Convent of the Incarnation in 1536. Teresa became so distressed by the too-comfortable life-style of the convent that she decided to found her own reformed convent in 1562. Slowly and painfully, her reform grew, ultimately confirmed by the Church as the Discalced Carmelites, of both women and men. Teresa of Avila was canonised in 1622, forty years after her death. Centuries later, after study of her extensive spiritual writing, Teresa was declared a Doctor of the Church.

In an earlier chapter, I cited Paul's experience of not doing what he says he wanted to do:

> *I do not understand my own actions.*
> *For I do not do what I want, but I do the very things I hate...*
> *I can will what is right, but I cannot do it.*
> *For I do not do the good I want,*
> *but the evil I do not want is what I do.*

Romans 7:15, 19

The ambivalent experience of wanting and not wanting the same thing at the same time, in fact, is fairly common. I recall a young fellow telling me how hard it was for him to take a risk. He gave numerous examples of courses of action which he had wanted to take, but had pulled back from because it felt like 'too big a risk'.

Paul attributes this to 'sin that dwells within me' (Romans 7:20). Which, more accurately, might be called my 'sinfulness' or my weakness. Rather, I call it the vulnerable spot in my make-up, where I am not entirely free in my inner life. As mentioned, we are essentially free people, indeed created free, but our experience is that our freedom is limited – I don't always do what I want to do. Effectively, we are *unfree*.

There are two telling examples in classical spiritual writing – from St Augustine and from St Teresa of Avila, both struggling with attractions in two opposite directions. Augustine tells of his struggle in his *Confessions*:

> *The two wills within me were in conflict and they tore my soul apart... I was quite sure that it was better for me to give myself up to your love than to surrender to my own lust. But while I wanted to follow the first course and was convinced that it was right, I was still a slave to the pleasures of the second. I had prayed to you for chastity and said 'Give me chastity and continence, but not yet'. For I was afraid that you would answer my prayer at once and cure me too soon of the diseases of lust, which I wanted satisfied, not quelled.*[33]

---

33 Augustine, *Confessions* (Harmondsworth, UK: Penguin, 1961), VIII, 5-7, 164-9.

Teresa's experience was different, but her struggle has many similarities:

> I was living an extremely burdensome life, because in prayer I understood more clearly my faults. On the one hand God was calling me, on the other hand I was following the world. All the things of God made me happy, those of the world held me bound. What a terrible mistake, God help me, that in wanting to be good, I withdrew from good.[34]

Teresa admitted that she didn't have the strength to move beyond what she named as some 'attachments' in her heart, not bad in themselves, but 'enough to spoil everything.'

Teresa describes her experience quite vividly in several places in her autobiography:

> I voyaged on this tempestuous sea for almost twenty years... I should say that it is one of the most painful lives... that one can imagine, for neither did I enjoy God, nor did I find happiness in the world.

> My soul was now tired; and, in spite of its desire, my wretched habits would not allow it to rest. Oh, God help me, how it frightens me, my soul's blindness despite so much assistance from God! It made me fearful to see how little I could do by myself and how bound I became, so that I was unable to resolve to give myself entirely to God.[35]

---

34 Teresa of Avila, 'The Book of Her Life' in Kieran Kavanaugh and Otilio Rodriguez, eds, *The Collected Works of St. Teresa of Avila*, (Washington DC: Institute of Carmelite Studies (1963), chapter 7.

35 Ibid., chapters 8 and 9.

In Augustine's and Teresa's experience, ambivalence is characterised by desire for one way yet apparent helplessness in relation to an opposite way. Teresa says she felt 'bound', unable to do anything herself to change the situation. This is the experience I call *unfreedom*.

We are unfree when we are 'attached'. Teresa tells us later that her attachment was to some friendships that she imagined that she could not live without:

> *What a terrible mistake, God help me, that in wanting to be good, I withdrew from good... Resolved to strive for purity of conscience and beseeching the Lord to help me, I saw, after trying it for some days, that my soul didn't have the strength to reach such perfection alone – on account of some attachments, that, though in themselves were not bad, were enough to spoil everything. My soul was not at all strong, but very fragile, especially with regard to giving up some friendships I had. Although I was not offending God by them, I was very attached.*[36]

Teresa of Avila did not have the advantage of today's psychology which would have offered her a deeper understanding of attachments. On an external level, she was attached to these friendships, but it is clear that some deeper, even unconscious, inner attachment underpinned the external attachment. Teresa was more likely attached to her deep need for affection, a need that was met in the friendships that were worrying her. My earlier friend who could not take risks, I suggest, was attached to some inner need for security

---

36 Ibid., chapter 23.

that constantly drew him in a direction opposite to what he really wanted.

Here is Teresa's description of how her ambivalence was resolved:

> One day entering the oratory I saw a statue they had borrowed for a certain feast to be celebrated in the house. It represented the much wounded Christ and was very devotional, so that beholding it, I was utterly distressed in seeing him that way... it seems to me, my heart broke... I threw myself down before him with the greatest outpouring of tears... I was very distrustful of myself and placed all my trust in God. I think I then said that I would not rise from there until he granted me what I was begging him for.
> (reading Augustine's Confessions) I remained for a long time totally dissolved in tears and feeling within myself utter distress and weariness. Oh, how a soul suffers, God help me, by losing the freedom it should have in being itself, and what torments it undergoes... May God be praised who gave me the life to rise up from a death so deadly.[37]

Again, Teresa emphasises her own powerlessness in the struggle and the invitation to trust God and wait on God's gift. The possibility of rising above our inner attachments or our *unfreedoms* comes as gift. Only God can set us free. When Paul asked God to take away the thorn in his flesh, it makes sense to us now that God said no, better to leave it there, for then you know the need for my grace. 'My grace is sufficient for you.' (2 Corinthians 12:9)

---

37 Ibid., chapter 9.

Once set free, no longer attached to her friendships, Teresa would have come to value her friendships more truly and enjoy them more gratefully.

Sebastian Moore

Sebastian Moore (1917-2014) was a Benedictine monk of Downside Abbey, UK. He was a progressive thinker, highly qualified in theology, but his teaching and writing were not always clear and were often questioned by other theologians. After a major disagreement with his Abbot, Moore spent twenty-one years teaching in American colleges in the aftermath of Vatican Council II. Moore spent his last years at Downside and died there in 2014.

In his celebrated play *Murder in the Cathedral*, T. S. Eliot has the Archbishop of Canterbury, Thomas Becket, preaching in his cathedral on Christmas morning in the year 1170.[38] Reflecting on the Mass of Christmas Day, the Archbishop notes that it is a celebration of both the birth of Our Lord and his passion and death on the cross – 'at the same time':

> *Whenever Mass is said, we celebrate the passion and death of Our Lord. On this Christmas Day, we do this in celebration of his birth... Beloved, as the world sees, this is to behave in a strange fashion. For who in the world will both mourn and rejoice at once and for the same reason? ... It is only in our*

---

38 T. S. Eliot, *Murder in the Cathedral* (London: Faber and Faber, 1965).

Christian mysteries that we can rejoice and mourn at once and for the same reason.

The Archbishop discusses this paradox of joy and sorrow at Christmas time and again in the death of martyrs, the following day being the feast of the first Christian martyr, St Stephen:

> *We do not think of a martyr simply as a good Christian who has been killed because he is a Christian: for that would be solely to mourn. We do not think of him simply as a good Christian who has been elevated to the company of the saints: for that would be simply to rejoice. And neither our mourning nor our rejoicing is as the world's is.*

Mourning alone would be unchristian; rejoicing alone would be inhuman. Rather, we rejoice and we mourn at the same time, and for the same reason.

Becket was murdered in his cathedral four days later, leaving his people with these words:

> *I do not think that I shall ever preach to you again. Because it is possible that in a short time you will have yet another martyr, and that one perhaps not the last. I would have you keep in your hearts these words that I say, and think of them at another time.*

Eliot highlights an essential element of true joy: sorrow and joy coexist. Sorrow and joy complement one another. Paradoxically, they belong together. Indeed, they are the basic Christian paradox: dying and rising.

This paradox is well captured in the image of the clown: the genuine clown lives the paradox of sadness and joy. Looking into the depth of a clown's eyes, I see an aloneness and a wholeness at once, at the same time. I am drawn more deeply into the *pathos*: though his face is sad, I find myself smiling! Sorrow and joy. I see the clown as the classic free person, totally free of self-interest. The clown is whole, makes no demands, is quite indifferent to people's reactions. It is no surprise that Jesus is often seen as a clown. In John's Gospel (19:5), Pilate presents Jesus to the crowds: Jesus is crowned, mocked, alone, to all appearances 'defeated' – *Ecce Homo* – but he remains silent, more self-assured than anyone else in the scene. There again is the paradox: Jesus' life is fulfilled in that moment of apparent defeat. That sounds foolish to me!

What makes for such inner freedom? I turn to Sebastian Moore who teaches that Jesus' total surrender to God, living in utter fidelity to his humanity, is the source of his deep freedom and love. He believes that, to understand one's true humanity, the starting point is the person of Jesus, not one's own limited experience of humanity. Because Jesus lived his humanity freely and fully, in complete authenticity, it is in relationship with Jesus that we discover the invitation to live an authentic life, born of freedom.

Moore paraphrases the hymn in Philippians 2:6-8 to capture Jesus' living his humanity faithfully and freely:

Jesus, being in the form of God (as all humans are)
did not translate this into being for himself (as all humans do),
but on the contrary took our humanness on in an

> extraordinary way,
> its true way, a way of total self-dispossession, of freedom
>   from ego,
> in which (upsetting all our ideas of what befits divinity)
> he made manifest the ultimate mystery
> that itself is poor, for-all, has no possessions, makes rank
>   meaningless...
> which fact became fully manifest in Jesus
> raised from the dead and receiving the name beyond
>   all names.[39]

For Moore, Paul was writing about Jesus' humanity, not his divinity, as some theologies teach. Jesus' 'emptying himself' was his choice to live his humanity fully and truly. This is humanity's 'true way', free of inner attachments, letting go of any self-focus or self-promotion. This is the way that Jesus lived, graced by God. Jesus' inner freedom makes possible his often-surprising choice of his disciples, his interaction with the Samaritan woman and others in his ministry, his silence before Pilate. There is no self-interest in Jesus.

I find support for this understanding of Jesus' living his humanity faithfully and fully in Jerome Murphy-O'Connor.[40] As I discussed fully in Set me Free,[41] Murphy-O'Connor presents Jesus' experience as the model of our living authentically.

39 Sebastian Moore, *Jesus, the Liberator of Desire* (New York: Crossroad, 1989), 42.

40 Jerome Murphy-O'Connor, *Becoming Human Together: The Pastoral Anthropology of St. Paul* (Wilmington DL: Michael Glazier Inc., 1982), 45ff.

41 Brian Gallagher, *Set me Free: Spiritual Direction and Discernment of Spirits* (Bayswater, Vic: Coventry Press, 2019).

He gives the analogy of one human person walking on the moon, another conquering Mount Everest and another running a mile in less than four minutes, achievements that were thought to be humanly impossible till one individual did the impossible. Since, many people have achieved the same feats. In one person's break-through, humanity knows the possibility. Murphy-O'Connor concludes that because Jesus lived his humanity truly and fully, then it is possible for all humanity.

Sebastian Moore recognises that, just as Jesus' oneness with God was the source of his freedom, so too the source of all people's freedom is oneness with God. The starting point is that God created all people free. God desires freedom for all and always works towards freedom for God's people. All people aspire to this freedom and know that, with grace, it is within reach, because of Jesus. The gift of God's grace is inner freedom, the fullness of humanity.

Conclusion

God's foolishness is wiser than human wisdom.

Human wisdom would have judged all of the people I have discussed as quite unready, ill-equipped for the roles they were given. Some seemed obviously unsuitable, as Teresa of Avila and Thomas Merton; some seemed out of place, insignificant in their lives, as Etty Hillesum and Jules Chevalier; some belonged in their monasteries, not on the road, as Constance Fitzgerald and Sebastian Moore.

God's foolishness, on the other hand, calls all of these women and men prophets, leaders, saints. The impact of their lives on people far and wide attests to the God-given wisdom they witnessed.

A lived spirituality of heart rests on all of the themes developed by these prophetic people. It is grounded in the conviction that God loves us first (Jules Chevalier's starting point), inviting us to trust that love, even in the more difficult experiences of our lives (emphasised by Teresa of Avila and Constance Fitzgerald). Living our lives fully and truly (prominent in the writings of Thomas Merton), as Jesus lived his life (taught by Sebastian Moore), then becomes possible for us and bears fruit in healthy loving relationships, committed to justice for all people (implied in all the writings, uppermost in Etty Hillesum and Martin Luther King, and affirmed by Lady Wisdom).

I honour these prophets, and I thank God for the gift that each one has been to me personally.

Some Reading

Anon. *The Cloud of Unknowing.* New York: Doubleday, 1973.

Etty Hillesum. *Letters from Westerbork,* ed. Jan G. Gaarlandt. London: Grafton Books, 1988.
Etty: a Diary 1941-1943. London: Triad Grafton Books, 1985.

John of the Cross. *Centered on Love: the Poems of St John of the Cross.* Translated by Marjorie Flower. Varroville NSW: the Carmelite Nuns, 1983, reprinted 2002.

Thomas Merton. *Contemplative Prayer.* New York: Herder & Herder, 1964.

Sebastian Moore. *The Inner Loneliness.* London: Darton, Longman & Todd, 1982.
Jesus, the Liberator of Desire. New York: Crossroad, 1989.

Teresa of Avila. *The Book of her Life,* in Kieran Kavanaugh and Otilio Rodriguez eds, *The Collected Works of St Teresa of Avila,* Washington, DC: Institute of Carmelite Studies, 1963.